THE INNER SELF
THE INNER STRENGTH

POETIC ENLIGHTENMENT FOR MOTIVATION

ALTHEA LEGISTER

authorHOUSE®

AuthorHouse™ UK
1663 Liberty Drive
Bloomington, IN 47403 USA
www.authorhouse.co.uk
Phone: 0800 047 8203 (Domestic TFN)
*   +44 1908 723714 (International)*

Published by AuthorHouse 11/04/2019

ISBN: 978-1-7283-9522-7 (sc)
ISBN: 978-1-7283-9521-0 (e)

Print information available on the last page.

Any people depicted in stock imagery provided by Getty Images are models, and such images are being used for illustrative purposes only. Certain stock imagery © Getty Images.

This book is printed on acid-free paper.

Because of the dynamic nature of the Internet, any web addresses or links contained in this book may have changed since publication and may no longer be valid. The views expressed in this work are solely those of the author and do not necessarily reflect the views of the publisher, and the publisher hereby disclaims any responsibility for them.

CONTENTS

All By Myself

I sit in a corner all by myself.
I spent lonely days and lonely nights resting in a vacuum,
a space that is meant for me.
I can see you hustling and bustling as busy as a bee!
When the time has come you put me down, my use is done.
I wave goodbye endlessly, and you
always dismiss me and leave me,
but with discerning eyes, I am eager to see
all that matters so randomly to me.

I Will

I will take time to smell the essence of life.
I will feel and feel.
I will seek and seek until I can find no more.
I will look at the stars.
I will follow my heart.
I will speak to the moon and be glad.
I will open my ears wide and listen
while the earth rumbles in tune.
I will see with my eyes what is meant to appear to me.
I will be thankful for all that my Creator has made for me.
I will not give up so very easily.
I will not be defeated as I am strong, beautiful and free.

Quick To Judge Another

Analyzation and assumptions aim at another man's
character while ignoring self-infliction of one's
shock of their own conceded mental state; Elation
and misconceptions of another man's misfortunes.
Liaise with mind and heart before you think
you have seen another man's inside.
Judge then, when you know that what the eyes see is the
truth of another man stain; because when life explodes in
your face and torment and malfunction heats your brain!
Only then you will feel and understand
another man's pain.
So judge no one yet until you are
attuned to your flaws first.

What Do I See

Looking in.
Looking out.
What do I see?
I see a little girl playing and having fun, laughing so happily with innocence glaring from her eyes.
I see a child with ideas and dreams unlived with stories that are yet to be told as big as her heart can be that will eventually unfold.
I see a teenager evolving subconsciously with hope, waiting to explore and unaware of reality, what is to come and what is to be.
I see a woman with plans and goals ready to fight for what she yearns with all her entirety.

Looking in.
Looking out.
What do I see?
I see broken dreams and failures but I also see hope and destiny.
I see warmth, love, and sincerity and I also see dept and honesty.
I see a giver, a lover, and a friend. A maker that works hard with compassion straight to the end.
I see a warrior within her rights and a survivor fighting for a cause and taking a stand.
I see bravery transcend with loyalty and a peaceful soul with modesty.

Looking in.
Looking out.
What do I see?
I see a Queen with a heart of gold and undeniable strength.
I see a fighter that conquers all with self-control, even with adversity she shines.
I see a winner that never gives up, she's a force to reckon with.
I see a proud and wonderful masterpiece, a mother's pride a mother's child.
I see all that is good from head to toes without a doubt in mind.
When I look in the mirror I see beauty transpired.
I see a woman that was made perfect and bold.

When You

When you realise that humanity doesn't have to be senseless.
We can change that, we can create the change we want it to be.
When you come to understand that as a human being we don't have to be lonely, and you realise that being selfless is not greed but being selfish makes you unfeeling to others needs.
When you know from within, you will always find a way to succeed and that unity gives strength as a team.
When you know that life is about fulfilling dreams, and it is also keeping it real on your toes, staying grounded in the sole of your feet.
When you have figured out that you are not alone, you are not an island nor or you a stone, so share and give some love because sometimes we all need a helping hand to reach our destinations and our goals.
Why do we make life so complex? when all it takes is me and you to be the change that will benefit all of us.
There is neither nor; or either-or; it is just simply showing care for our own humane lives when we know that life belongs to all.

Too Many Times

Too many times.
I can't do it, no more.
I have been left with so much pain; always being
left to cope on my own, to pick up the pieces of
yours and my growing pains and I never gained.
Only from the insight of my pain, I learnt
many lessons along the way.
I can't take it anymore!
So, I have decided to stay on my own; to protect
my womb from suffering in silence, that bear
the weight of my treacherous moments.
So, I have decided to shield myself and guarded my
soul against a broken spirit and a broken heart.
Too much and too long I have longed to be with
someone who will love me for who I am.
Someone who will add to my happiness and
not leave me angry and desolate.
I have gone down that road too many times, starting over
again and again with the feeling I had done something
wrong when I all I needed was love and compassion.
Too many times, although I have walked a different
path my heart gets broken too many times.
It took me the courage to realise that my-self is all I got.
With that in mind, I will not look back because
too many times has stabbed me in my back.
Trusting chances that I have taken with the ones
I thought would love me and have my back.
In the end, it doesn't take me long to find out that I had
no one until when I needed help they turn their backs.
I am all I got.
Too many times is too much.
It's a lot.

The Greatest Version

The greatest version of myself is depleting my inner self of the negative
traits I was programmed to assume, I was limited to living my best life.
Hence, I now realise that what is beyond me is not just
a messy, fleshy self but a spirit that thinks deep and
wide, beyond her years but never knew why.
Yet, the feeling of knowing was there inside of me. I knew there was
something strange happening to my existence but I didn't know
the universe had a plan to rescue me from my misery; Confusion
and isolation was part of my barriers but now I know why.

When life takes you through the whoops, "you know that pain that you
feel when your mind ain't right?" the frustration that you feel when the
directions you are heading in your life ain't so clear? It just doesn't feel right!

So I took it upon myself to fix what doesn't feel right, then I realised, I am
alive and I am not just a living breathing thing that sleeps through the night!
The moment I began my journey of soul reflection, it became
clear to me that I was living my life in a shell full of lies. To
add to that; I was told all my life that "practice makes perfect"
but then, I wasn't told to practice my mind right!
Yes, it is interesting to know that once I started getting my mind
right the mental disease of negative thinking diminish slowly
while like a caterpillar I change into a radiant butterfly.

The greatest version of self is harmonising the song inside of you
that tells you who you are, listening to the voice that speaks from
a distance from the core of your gut to the heart of your soul.
Yes! The change begins with you and it starts from within.

I once use to blame God and everything else outside of me when my mind
wasn't right but now I can make excuses for that state of mind; now that I
know I was suffering from a mental prolapse. When depression took its toll
I almost gave in and I almost gave up but then I realised that it was a test.
I told myself I am not heading down that road and then
my mind started changing into a positive glow.
If your gut inside of you feels strange and your mind is confused
then that is telling you something isn't right, so fix it.

I started to realise that to become the great, greater and greatest version
of myself, I had to get rid of a filthy, junky mindset that drains away
from the substance in my body that I never get to recharge like a battery.
I knew that something had to change inside of me to become who I was
meant to be. It is not about materialism, neither is it about egotism, it
has always been for me about mind, body, and soul, So if your mind
is right and your six chakras synchronized with your mind's eye then
you will know what becoming your greatest version feels like.

I Am An Individual

I am an individual.
I am kind, lovable and caring.
I am strong, brave and determined.
I tell myself that these traits are a part of me.
It doesn't stop there!
There is a lot more to me.

I am hopeful and resilient.
I bounce back if I have to, it doesn't end there.
I am a dreamer with great ambitions.
I know life has no limitations but only if I put boundaries
in my way.
I have faith in my existence.

I rely on my true nature and good intentions.
I am connected with my universe, to whom I give my
honour.
I am loved by my creator who gave me a beautiful soul
to relish in my favour.
I am unique and distinctive, however, I will end on this
note.
I can create great things as I use my intellect to build
with joy and pleasure.
I am different.
I am me.
I do not compare to no other.

Broken Relationships

If only we know the pain we cause when we deceive another soul and the lies
we tell are so bold our relationships end up turning cold.
It may be a joke to a lot of fools who may think that they have caught just
another fish from the sea but when the relationship becomes harder to please
they run away from the responsibility they don't want to keep.
They may think they earn their rights automatically when you open your arms and
welcome a kiss on the cheek, then you open your heart as you feel this is the one to
keep, this is real, but as deception takes its toll they forgot that they were happy to
enter your life but forgot that was the case and then decide when to leave.

Left alone to figure things out is like hanging on the wall like a frame.
With dismay you wondered what had happened, how can this be! things are not
the same.
After all, that time and effort spent loving someone instead of loving self more,
your energy is drained.
Finding the courage to start all over again and once more, one may wonder
why one is left in such hostile place with resentment and lost hope because the
relationship didn't work out in that time and space.

One may think it's over but it is not so.
It is over because that person is meant to go.
Sometimes we make mistakes along the way by choosing the ones we think
loves us so much, and when they turn around and hurt us we question things we
do not know.
We wonder why they go when we thought they love us so but the universe will
always respond to us in ways for us to learn, but it is down to us to make that
U-Turn.

Our hearts may be broken but love is like a token.
With life comes, an abundance of choices and awareness is gained through our
experiences.
Don't feel like a pillock or feel ashamed.
It is just a part of life we have to embrace like a game as broken relationships are
just a matter that is waiting to shape or form to build yourself to the next stage.

Change

Times are changing.
As we get older we are growing with time.
The world is changing around us.
As children in the world we once knew is not the world we grow up to see.
Events are unfolding before our eyes but are we seeing, observing and feeling what is happening?
When will you change?

Will your life change when you sit, wait and wonder?
Then ponder about the things that distract us from evolving!
Do you think you are doing enough to solve the matter?
Do you feel like you are living your purpose, your best life or do you feel like you are just existing!
When you change the world will change around you.

When you see, feel and hear different views, change thoughts and become new then the mind will open to receive and the spirit inside you will become awake because if you are stuck to one set of thinking and keep the same mindset rolling then will you ever explore what is on offer to you?

The Creator does not sit on a throne to watch you stumble, suffer and moan or to allow you to be confused and weak. The "Most High" speaks to you through your karmas and gives clues to reinforce life's dramas.
Learn the lessons and move on as that is where part of your change lies.
Change yourself first if you want a change.
Change begins with you from within.
It starts with you.

Don't waste energy on silly things and then in-turn expects the world to owe you something.
In time, when you create the change in you; you will see the beauty that it brings.
Life is about abundance of everything and anything but it is down to you and each one of us to make that abundance fulfilling and sharing love is a beginning; as once we let go of the things we do not need then the universe will step in and guide us and help to bring the change we need.

Change what you can, don't bombard yourself with unnecessary junk because life is beautiful inside and out,
but when we show gratitude to life itself and love ourselves then we will see the beauty and love that life has to give.
This might be hard for some to do because we are so caught up with things that do not apply to us, nor or they truth but if we look back and think: ask yourself or ourselves this question, do I need these things?
Then you will see that the question answers itself.

Change begins with oneself.

When you change, when I change, when we change then the world will change too.

Through Adversity

Through adversity, I strive.
I take pride in my steps as I rise.
Through adversity, I dream to be my best in my quest to deliver my aim with zest.
Through adversity, I shall become the proud and eager warrior as I am tested with time.
I will shine and I will fight for what is mine.
Through adversity, I will conquer all that my heart desire and until then I will not retire.
I will not shatter my flaws and give up at all.
Through adversity, I will become one with my all and I will stand tall.
Through adversity, I have the power to condemn my thoughts that keeps away the joy and tells me I am a failure and fear is my keeper.
Through adversity, I may be disappointed at times but I am resilient even when I cry.
I will not be devoured and swallowed up by the force of my flesh.
Through adversity, I will fight and fight even with my last breath.
I will not give up, I will keep trying until I die.
Through adversity, I will forever be victorious as failure is not a choice.
It does not exist in my eyes.
It is just a myth with no real truth to it.

The Eagle

Have you ever seen an eagle soar?
Soar to great heights as it roams the skies!
Looking for preys above the land!
Flying as high as it proudly stands.
Bracing itself as it zooms along with the clouds, beneath the
skies with its eyes setting traps as it wonders on.
With a cunning approach like a sly fox, the eagle is getting
ready to strike back!
As it fiercely reckons with its other foes while searching for
food as hunger approach.
Its stomach churns while it plots and waits keenly, to launch as
its target awaits.
It grips its claws in and leaps defiantly, with bold intent.

The moment has come for the time to eat.
Survival is key for the hungry eagle, it is getting ready to leap.
It doesn't care any longer and it did not sleep.
Aiming bravely, and preparing to jump!
Run victim! Run! The victim has tried but not much hope left in
sight!
The victim has now become food for the skies.
Given no chance to run very far for progress, life has ended
and the eagle has caught its target.
Probably, breathless once completed its disguise.
Again! The Eagle has won.
The Master of the skies.

When The Clouds Move

When the clouds move.
There is a bigger surface underneath, something we very
rarely notice and a picture we do not take the time to see.
Above the surface, below the surface, in between,
layers of thicken fogs looking bulky as they steep.
Separating and disintegrating as the clouds move
away, the grey skies, the blue skies and the white
skies shine their bright light in the day.
In different directions, you can see a bigger cloud underneath.

Beyond the skies, what do I see?
Clouds moving slowly, how fascinating! This is beyond me.
There is a light that shines, it gives us vitamin D.
The big blue skies have so much intention that when you look
up you would not realise how perfect we are meant to be.

If you don't pay attention you would not see what
the clouds have to offer to you and me.
I wonder how many different types of clouds are up there to see?
Different clusters appearing, what a sight to see.
It proves and shows that nothing stay still as even
the clouds changes when nature steps in.
The moving clouds move along and change
its directions as it is required to be.
Just like you and me.

The Rainbow

The seven colours of the rainbow.
Swept away by the daylight sun.
They fade with memories over the mountaintop.
With sunshine rays, they sparkle and shine in the fog.
Like brightly coloured ribbons they curved around the hills.
They give hope and glow with the daffodils.
The rainbow engulfs the atmosphere as its beauty transcends with
hope.
The seven colours of the rainbow protruded through the air and
will always be here regardless of when they choose to appear.
Nature is so beautiful even when it is not noticed but it is important
to be grateful even when the rainbow has vanished.
The rainbow may disappear in time but only when it has done its
time.
The seven colours of the rainbow can distinguish between rain or
shine, but that's its purpose to decide.
It can decide when to stay or when to go. It is the ruler of its sign.
It gives the message that humankind is not alone and guided by the
mysteries of life existence throughout time.

Ups And Downs

Life has its ups and downs.
Sometimes it can feel like a storm,
but amid all that storm, you just
have to keep moving on.
Keep rolling on and tumbling, even if
you feel as if you are not moving.
Even when you think and feel like
there is no point, you're struggling,
and you feel like you are drowning.
Keep swimming because if you stop, you
might as well give up or the wind and
the tides will just swallow you up.

Be Grateful For The Rain

Be grateful for the rain.
Do not complain.
A shower of rain is blissful in disguise.
It brings a surprise.
Thunder roars while lightning flashes with a magical
glow.
The storm comes, but then at rest becomes a steady flow.
It calms the earth after the rush.
Then bring to shore quietness and stillness that's good for
the soul.
When the ripples of the sea flow and flow, the beauty it
shows.

Be grateful for the rain.
Do not complain.
It cleans and goes where the still water flows.
The rivers, the mountains, and the springs will appreciate
the silence after the roar.
Sometimes it makes the sky grey, sometimes it makes the
clouds move.
But after havoc comes peaceful days.
When the rainbow appears with red, yellow, green,
orange, blue, indigo, and violet too, the colours combined
is not a mistake, it is just a note to say I care for you.
When nature calls, the rain has to pour.
So appreciate and be grateful for the rain.

I See The Wonders

As I walk the streets at nights, I can see the pillars rise.
I seek solitude from the night skies.
The moon eclipse and gave me teary eyes.
As I looked up in the skies, I see the stars shine their light.
The planets transformed and change their orbits twice.
I thought it was imagination.
I saw that it was realisation.
The scenery was not an illusion.
I saw the clouds moving.
I thought that they were roaring.
The darkness kept canoeing in the middle of the night.
I knew they were not spears.
I knew it was not magic as there are flashes in the skies.
It was a clear sight.
I could see bright lights, as I looked up in awe and saw that it was just the wonders of nature and life.

Somebody's Child

Somebody's child is somebody's cry.
A mother's child is a mother's cry.
A father's child is a father's pride.
Someday somebody's child will tell their story; how it feels to be a mother, to be a father, to be a grandmother and to be a grandfather.
They will tell you how it feels to be an aunt, to be an uncle, to be a sister and to be a brother.
They will also tell you how it feels to be a niece, to be nephew, to be granddaughter and to be a grandson.

As the list goes on it is very clear that we are all somebody's child, but why is this unidentifiable when the homeless are always in need? They live a life that is empty and in a world that is full of greed, and why do they suffer from lack when there is so much food that is thrown away on the streets!

Why is this unidentifiable when the crippled are looked down at because they may look different as if they come from a different creed!

Why is this unidentifiable when the abusers become abused and the abuse become abusers because they are just so confused as to whom they are meant to be.

Why is this unidentifiable when the lonely get depressed they reach out for help by talking so much when you show some kindness, but get dismissed when the conversation is done because it seems pointless!

In all these scenarios somebody's child is suffering in silence, so why do we become so selfish and feel it is none of our business while each day somebody's child is hurting we turn our backs like it is nothing.

We ignore the fact that everyone matters just like us and that each one teaches one can help each one to give a helping hand. So often somebody's child gets dismissed and we pretend that they have no feelings but in the end, we cry for them when destruction creeps in.

When will humanity ever learn that its purpose is diverse and is not meant to be stuck in one place? When somebody's child is affected there is a conscious connection we might not comprehend as we are caught up in our feelings, that somebody's else's child does not matter because some people think that existence is just, an individual thing.

It Is Ok

It is ok to feel like you don't have to please everyone, and it is also ok to put yourself in the centre of your world.

It is ok to admit that you are wrong, after all, no one is all perfection.

It is ok to be you, what do you have to lose?

It is ok to put a smile on your heart even when it seems too hard to do.

It is ok to cry when you feel like it, tears are like a fountain you have to release it.

It is ok to also try, if you feel like you are falling, keep pushing, brush off your knees if you fall on them and then get up and walk again.

It is ok to fail now and then, as a matter of fact, there is nothing as such but if you make it so, it will become as such.

It is ok to give a helping hand, when you do someone will help you back in just a glance.

It is ok to show some kindness, it doesn't hurt because it can help you in the end, to be kinder to your self.

It is ok to feel sadness because sometimes life can seem unfair but don't become a host for hopelessness.

It is ok to laugh now and then, it can keep lines and wrinkles off your face even when sometimes that is not the case.

It is ok to tell others how we feel, it takes courage at times but at least they will know that you feel.

It is ok to tell others we love them because it shows we can love ourselves enough to share the love with others in need.

It is ok to give some hugs, it shows that you love the warmth and you can feel.

It is ok to set some boundaries because your life is yours and you have to live it as it is real.

It is ok to take deep breaths when life becomes all too much to deal with, which sometimes can be surreal.

It is ok to tell yourself, I am ok and I am important.

I am ecstatic, I am special and I can do this.

Her Logical Mind

*Her logical mind can be redefined by all that seems impossible inside the mind.
From time to time her views may seem inadequate but her strength relates to her senses untouched.
With no limitations, her eyes can see things when she imagined far beyond.
She can feel what she hasn't touched and create with her mind and heart if she needs to and if it is relevant.
Her logical mind gives her comfort and put her at rest when she already knows her side of the test.
The mind of her soul wonders, it may wobble or it may stretch but whatever it does her energy will be harnessed.
It gives her bliss when she understands the potential of her character that has the power to create what her heart desires.
It may seem heartless when she doesn't think less of herself but instead focuses on her greatness.
Her logical mind helps her even when she seems emotionless, she still gives all her love with truth and strives to be the best in whatever role she chose to play with kindness.
She is the best. She is proud and she is smart and she is gracefully effortless.
She holds her persona fiercely, and she is flexible in her thoughts.
She is not a pushover, she owns her life the way she owns her mind.
It is the love she has for herself that gives her the strength to combat all her fights.
She is a lover of life but also a sensitive soul with great insights.*

Insanity

You came into my life; you made me cry.
You made me hoped for another life.
You made me imagined I was lost, and I was nothing more than an
empty shell.
You looked me in the face and lied.
You told me, I had no worth and I was sad.

You gave me visions in the mornings and late at nights.
You made me think I was useless and deserve not much in life.
You pushed me, poked me and pinched me, I screamed in agony!
You made me feel as if I was the only one in the world that was bad
beyond compare.
You told me I was mad and my life is a drag, I was fearful and terrified
in my mind.

Insanity.
You gave me doubts, I wasn't brave to see that the thoughts you gave
weren't true.
You made me promises and they were false.
You took away my freedom and showed me no love, despair was all
that seem to appear.
Bye, bye insanity,
I am now happy, I got your point.
Without you, I would have never learnt lessons I needed to learn to
break freely away
from you.
You opened my eyes to see how heartless you can be.
Thank you for the journey that you showed to me.
With dreaded memories, I am now free.

Bye, bye insanity.
You stayed around long enough and showed you are enraged.
I must say goodbye as you are not the kind of friend I want in my life,
neither do I want to be or see.
Bye, bye insanity.
You gave me a story that was meant for me.
Thank you for the lessons you have given to me.

My Sister And I

My sister and I, the outcast of a man.
We struggled, and we tried with tears in our eyes.
Through tested times, through thick and thin we stick together.
Left and right we swayed together, like windy leaves.
We capture in love yet no one sees that it is because we are one
why our bond is so precious.
We understand each other as we have the same desire, to love and
be loved by our one and only father.
There is no compensation for what we yearn for but only the
Creator knows what we cannot see.
The strife and pain he feels is the need of love that he cannot give.
So let it be my best friend as it is the Creator that knows the truth
of our pain.
Let thy father be as he will not understand that he desires the same
compassion that he denies you and me.

Thick Skin

Thick Skin.
Where have you been?
You seldom approach me!
You seldomly come in.
I know I am not a coward.
I know I am not afraid, but oftentimes, I think I get left on my own
time and time again.
With you in mind, I tend to find the courage to start all over again.
Even when others say I have no chance to win and I am useless,
but I never give in.
With all this nonsense you would always step in.
You would tell me, "don't mind them, I will keep you guided as
their opinions will always be endless!"
So where are you? I am trying to find my thick skin.
I know you keep my company from within so show me evidence
that you are in.
I have missed you.
You have gone too long.
I am tired of all the rejection and criticism.
I try to be brave and to fit in but it is not working, I am still
drifting.
In spite of this, I know you are there waiting for me to find my thick
skin, so help me.
I need to find the fight from within.

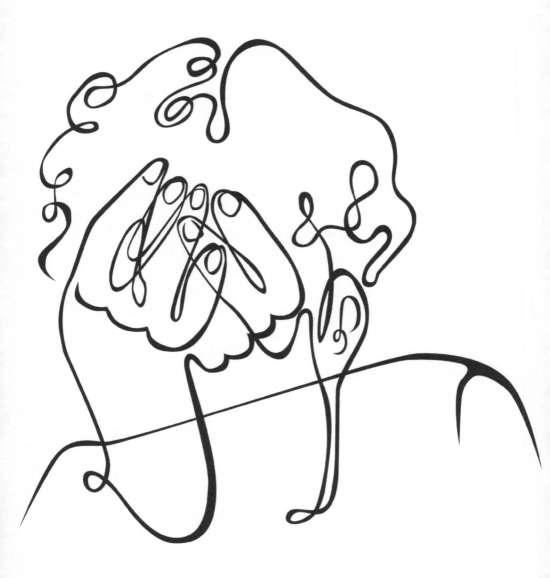

Depression

I thought it was normal when I felt sad.
I didn't know what it was like anymore to feel glad.
I felt numb in places, I didn't understand.
I blamed my emotions when I cried a lot.
It took me a while to realise it was more than that.

I didn't know I was living a lie when fear sets in and made me want to die.
My body was filled with aches and pains and I thought that was normal.
I thought if I ignored it then all that would pass.
I could not explain why all the faults I found with self was keeping me subdued.
I could not explain why I was so angry and sad, I didn't know what to do.
Then I realised it can't be true, there has to be much more to life than these wretched few.

I woke up in the mornings and felt drained and I didn't know it was because of my head pain.
The echoes in my head kept saying no, this is normal so don't go.
I forced myself to move to the other side of the bed, then I heard a voice said, "get up you need to go, so force yourself to do so!"
Over and over again, I heard the voice kept shouting in my head until I found the courage and said,
"yes, I know it is that time again!".

I felt alone in myself and I couldn't find a way to break out of that cell.
It felt like I was in hell, I kept a smile on my face and they thought I was well.
I tried to explain that I was only putting on a brave face and I didn't feel well, but they thought I was joking and told me to get on with it, what I am saying does not make sense.
So I kept on pushing and plodding along as if nothing has happened.
I was fooling myself, that is what they said.

One day I decided that there has to be a solution, this doesn't feel right, why do I feel bad and why do I feel like I want to go mad, then my doctor decided that Prozac was the answer.
I said no! I am the cause of my actions, I will think good thoughts and change the matter.
There is no way I would allow my life to be taken over by the mind that is corrupted and hurting my soul. It is unfriendly and very cold. A heartless thing that wants to control. If I had allowed it, it would have consumed me as a whole.

I knew that perceptions needed to be changed and new concepts needed to be gained.
My body was doing one thing and my mind was in a state, I had to figure out how to relate.
I wouldn't have imagined even until today how powerful my mind was focused on making me sway.
Depression is real. It is not a myth and it doesn't wait for you, it comes and goes as it pleases, sometimes it stays around for a very long time, overstay its visit and it doesn't want you to know that it truly exists. It will tell you it is ok to feel like this: lonely, sad, confused, tired and blue so don't accept it.

The Bullies

There are issues here and there are issues there if the bullies say they don't care.
There will be problems everywhere if the bullies say they don't care.
They become their nightmares with his or her thoughts but never mind them!
They will only embark on a misguided path that they forget is there.

They are high profile savages that are within their status quo, that in their minds they fool themselves because they actually, think it is so.
A bully never sees down the road because the bully is too busy thinking of whom is next to control.
Their attitude shows that they think they own the world and they may feel like they are having a grandeur experience with their shifty camouflage when in fact they are just hiding from their faults.

They will fight to combat raw cutting edges that grazed the minds of their self-inflicting madness when all it takes is to deal with their sadness.
Their attitude discloses maliciousness but the bullies would never realise the effect that they cause when they arm another soul because they are too busy with creating havoc and unhappiness.

They never learn until when it is too late, they say, "I am sorry, I have made a mistake." Usually, in this case, their victim is dead by the time an apology is said or if the victim is a fighter within themselves they will survive their afflicter affliction and stand proudly once they strive to love themselves.

When their wrongs defile them and they are defeated, the bully, if they have a conscience, they become the victim themselves more or less as they eventually try to take control of their mess but the ones who have decided to forgive them will become the ones that are victimless.

My Father And My Mother

My father never knew.
He never understood how he was meant to treat his
child as a shining star. I never gave up.
I pushed myself to a great extent to reach
the sky, the moon, and the stars.
Without my father's help, I realised that I am a star within
my rights as I tried in many ways to become the greatest
version of myself in spite of my father's faults.
He did not realise I would get that far. He thought I
was joking when I insisted I am going to shine and
through his eyes, I gave him a surprise from afar.

My mother knew I had ambitions and she never doubted me at all.
She gave me hope and encouraged me to be my best, at all.
In spite of my mother's ways she always understood what it
takes to allow a child to grow and succeed with no mistakes.
If I could choose out of the two, I would be lying
to myself and I would be confused.
They are different in many ways but there is nothing I can do.
I take pride in whatever I do and I think it is because of those two.
They created me and that's the truth no matter what I say or do.
It's just that my mother and my father will always have
something to say to me regardless of what I anticipate.

No matter what their opinions are they can choose to inspire
me and I learn from what I see. Sometimes they press my
buttons, they make me angry and I wish I didn't have to cry.
My father would say, "No matter how old you are, I am always
going to be your father and you are always going to be my child."
My mother would say, "I gave birth to you and no matter
what you do I am still your mother, so listen and learn and
don't be stubborn, you will always be my child."

What can I say!
I was formed from the two, even if they turned me black or
blue, I still have to accept that it is true. There is a reason
they are my parents and there is nothing I can do. So I choose
to give love and hug them and just shake my head too.

Tears

I woke up this morning pretending.
Pretending as if I was not hurting.
Deep down I know there is no escape but I kept deviating from the emotions that I am feeling.
It is not a case of wanting to explore my feelings while the need to cry is overbearing.
I just make it my duty to tell myself that it will be fine! It is just a phase of knowing.
I am not alright but I continued plodding.
I tried to think of nothing but ended up with something that keeps me going.
Staying positive and fighting with the will to avoid complex situations that I cannot comprehend.
Compromise does not work in my favour but I tried because I feel it matters.
Even when emotions come tumbling, I can feel my tears boiling, waiting to flow over like a boiling pot running over, but I tell myself it will not last forever.

The Ego

The ego is too big.
I have no time for that senseless thing!
The ego is too big.
It waste energy and makes you feel ill.
The ego is like a roaring lion, it is proud and fiercely brave.
When it takes over it gives you goosebumps and chills.
It can turn you into a pillock and make you feel stupid after the thrill.
The ego doesn't care, it just wants you to know that "I am here, look
at me!" It will say, in a boastful way. "I am the best thing on earth no
matter what you say."

The ego knows when you are weak and then embarrassed you even in
the streets.
The ego stops you from learning, It will make you ignorant and turns
you bleak.
The ego thinks that arrogance is the best thing for you when in fact it
is hindering you from being intact.
The ego cannot wait to see you fall, it propels you to do a recall.
It takes over your emotions, your sense of self and makes you think
you are doing well and standing for a good cause.

They say that "ignorance is bliss," but then your ego already knows
this.
Take care of your ego before you crash and burn.
It can tarnish your image and make you feel shame, making you feel
obsolete with no manners and etiquette, your ego thinks that it is a
game.
The ego is not always your best friend unless you use it positively.
It gives you false hope and tells you it is ok.
The ego doesn't play and It can make you lose good friends along the
way, it can even make you think it is them that gives the friendship
away.
The ego laughs, and laughs, and laughs, ha, ha, ha, ha, in your face
and then tells you are a disgrace.

Behind The Smiles

Behind the smiles of many folks, there is a willingness to survive.
Behind the smiles, there is a fight to live, to be better and most of
all to exist.
As life breathes and with the breath it gives it yearns to exist in the
being of its host.
Behind the smiles, there are pain and suffering, heartaches and no
hope.
Behind the smiles, there are resentments, strife and shame in the
faces of the ones that don't say much.

Behind the smiles of many folks, some faces show strength and
pride in spite of their story they haven't told.
The faces that fight to heal their wounds and they cover and
disguise their scars with a smile.

Behind the smiles, many souls are hungry for options and they
thirst for love from afar.
Behind the smiles, deep down they wished for joy, peace and
happiness but cannot find it.
They smile with pain in their hearts but yet they show courage as
they find the strength to be strong and courageous in public.

Behind the smiles, they make that choice to forgive themselves, as
it is easier to do than to feel helpless and as if they are not worth it.
They choose to hide behind the smiles as it is a lot better to deal
with than to walk around with tears in their eyes and with their
many cries while they are still trying to find their true purpose.

The Neighbour

The neighbour next door.
We greeted each other, in which I noticed we became friendly also.
In just a matter of time, we became a team and I became a friend
that my neighbour sees.
With pleasantness, we laugh as we speak with each other over the
picket fence.
The stories were told there and then, and it reminds me of how
funny we can be.
We looked out for our foes and give a command, when danger sets
in we rang the alarm.
We give cheer to each other and give strength and courage to the
company we possess.
Until one day I asked myself, "where is my neighbour?"
Is it a holiday or a vacation! there was no presence for many days.
The front yard of the house needs to be cut in edges.
The summer is here and the grass isn't cut as yet! I wondered in
dismay.
Where has my neighbour gone to stay?
Until one day I asked to borrow a spade then I was told my
neighbour had passed away.
I was shocked to my core, I wanted to cry.
I felt as I was missing a part of my leg as I lean to the side.
I picked up the courage to say goodbye.
It was hard to accept and I felt very sad.
My neighbour is dead, I can't believe my neighbour is gone.
My neighbour had passed on.
For some time, I denied reality and felt alone inside myself.
I felt sad for many days and I couldn't resist the thought of not
seeing my neighbour's smiles again.
The memories still live on in my mind.
As time went by, I continued, and I tried to accept that I will never
see my lovely neighbour's face again.

Black Rose

Beautiful black rose.
Your features are so bizarre!
You are so exotic.
Your petals are so soft and your fringe feels like pearls.
You are awesomely fascinating and your green vines are so
delicate.
Your buds open up so sprightly!
You are so lovely.
You blossom and curl.
You bloom with affection.
The mist of the air makes your leaves wet with sleet.
Your velvet skin feels subtle and sleek.

Your beauty beholds me, I am gripped by your charm.
Why do I see such beauty in the darkness you possess?
You are humbly interesting, What can I say! I am deeply obsessed.
I admire you.
You are one of a kind.
You are so intricate and yet so divine.
I will not forget your beauty, as I hold you close, I smell your
fragrance through my nose.
Your beauty makes me smile and gives me comfort as it may.
With your tender touch, your memories will be with me forever
and always.
You are a beautiful black rose.

The Box

Sometimes in life, you have to store your life in a box.
You don't have to forget about what you have been through and all the obstacles that you have faced.
The box is just there to help you to realise that life has its tendencies to heal or make you break.
Your pain will either make you weaker or stronger and prepare you for more experiences in a better way, but only if you have learnt and mastered lessons along the way.

The box, is a tool, an imaginary tool that can be used to help with dealing with life positively.
You don't have to carry the burdens of your mistakes and forget about living your best life when you are here to experience life anyways.
Remember that you are your spirit inside of your body. You can go, explore and be anywhere!
So, why tell yourself that you are only defined to just one place which is in your mind!
You can always go back to that box when you feel like it, and remember, things don't have to stay the same, it can always change.

The box may contain your emotions but a least it can help you to get in motion.
It can push and propel you in different directions but then you will be learning the art of moving along and moving on.
The box can do great things, it can even inspire you to be a better person.
You can change your circumstances, you can analyze deeply, reflect and have self-control of your existence.

You don't have to live your life holding on to guilt and shame.
You don't have to live your life stubbornly with hate and reject those who want you to gain. So, put your stuff in a box. You can choose to pick it up now and then or if you wish you can choose to get a new box and start again, it is up to you.
So whatever you do, even if you don't know what to do with your past and previous pains, just get a box and store them inside. Put it in a corner and wait for transformation. It will happen, even before you know it. You will get there.

Time

What is Time?
Is it seconds, minutes and hours?
Is it days, weeks, months and years?
What is time!
The clocks ticks and ticks away!
Tick, tock.
Tick, tock.
Tick, tock.
Tick, tock.
Tick, tock.
But the less value that is placed on time eventually becomes the same value that we placed on our lives.
It is precious to our souls and we cannot bargain once we get old.
It cannot be replaced and neither can it be re-traced.
It comes and goes and will disappear into thin air and vanishes away like it never existed but with gathered thoughts, only memories will unfold.
It is the master of existence that counteracts our expressions and actions.
It is a requisition that brings order to life whether new or old.
It is a healer that heals when there is a need to move on from the past while subsiding pain dissolved.
It is a teacher that teaches many lessons that need to be learnt in various and different ways.
It is a giver that gives what is due and also a taker that shows that karma is true.
It is a decision-maker that determines now factors and goals but only you can decide depending on the path you choose.
It is a creator that paints a picture of where you need to be as it mends broken hearts and fixes the past.
It gives a chance to build your self-esteem and to work on aspects you need to improve.
It adjusts and amends your life lessons so that you can learn from your experience and it gives you a chance to use your opportunities as a tool.
It shapes and fixes and bends as it is flexible for you to use.
It reaches and it touches and allows you to feel what cannot be ignored,
It is genuine and no one can escape it as everyone timing is different but we all have a purpose, whether to serve or to lead.
It enables you to see and feel the depth of love and hate but also to cover your wounds and take you to a different place.
It is fair and does not condone limitations in life itself as it gives a chance for change, development and growth.
It can show all these options but you have the choice to accept when the time is right for you.
Time may be enclosed in a clock frame but it is more than just a second hand, a minute hand and an hour hand that moves.

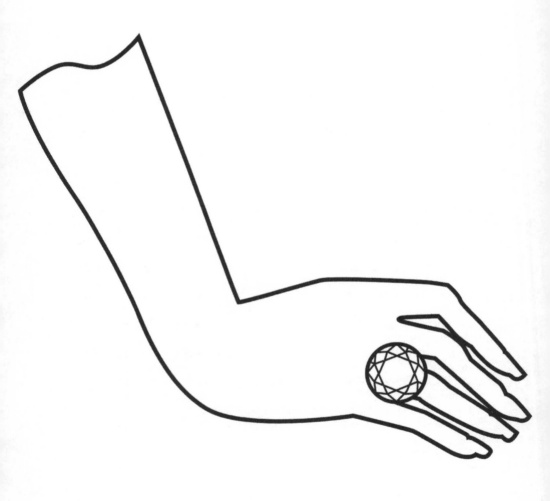

The Silver Ring

The silver ring, inside and out it sparkles and shines
With a diamond in between, it also has a sign engraved
with a rhyme saying I love you and you are mine.
It is genuine and solemnly beautiful.
I can tell that it was created with love in mind.
It has a lovely sheen and also very refined.
I don't know much about silver rings but I
know this one put twinkles in my eyes.
It may seem strange about what I am saying
but it matters tremendously to me.
This ring is made especially for me, it is certainly mine.
It is special in my eyes and I like the way it feels.
It might not have cost a great amount but it is
the thought that counts as I appreciate the little
things in life and what life has to give.
It is surreal to find a ring that is so unique
and there is no other like it.
It is not about the quantity of its kind; it seems
like this one was made with me in mind.
It stands out to me more than the rest and
that is how I know it's mine.
It feels like love at first sight, it brings joy to my eyes.
As I see the silver glows, the ring changes its course, the
shining wavered up and down in the sun the most.

The moral of the story is no matter where you are;
no matter what you do and no matter where you
go Life will bring opportunities right to you.
Whatever is for you will be for you and sometime
it will pop up right out of the blue.
Whether it is a seashell or a pine cone it doesn't matter what
your circumstances are, what is for you will always find you.

If The Skies Turn Black

If the skies turn black!
What would I do next?
I would feel my heartbeat.
I know, I would struggle to breathe.
If I were not strong enough, I would feel much more than shock.
If I were to run or hide away from the darkness, I cannot imagine that.
Just where would I go if the skies turn black?

The darkness would grip me, I know for sure.
I would stand still and wait for mercy.
I would think the end is here!
I would feel my worst fear.
I would jump out of my skin and shiver from within.

If the skies turn black.
I would not wait on my knees as I know there would be not much need to
say how I feel, there would not be much more time for that.
If the skies turn black right before my eyes, I think I would freeze!

If I had spent all my time dwindling throughout my life, then I would
know that the darkness wouldn't be a surprise.
My soul would be ready to accept the darkness if I had worked on my
reflex.
Reflecting and preparing for the darkness of the subconscious, then if
there is a rapture, I would know my effort wasn't useless and I would
know how to face the darkness.

If I had felt captured in my body it would feel like a trap standing frozen
with a silent heart attack, if I had spent my life being faithless when I
didn't give a toss or care for what is next.
So what if the skies should turn black, is it possible! am I crazy to think
that?
What if the skies turn black, what would I do to be exact?
How would I handle the darkness or would I just die on the spot?
What if the skies should turn black?
I wouldn't want to imagine that.

The Bottle

The bottle that holds the special things.
No matter where it goes it will never sink.
It floats on water if it is light within and contains
the contents that will keep it still.
Only on its terms it will glide or spill or if it is
swept away by the tide of its surrounding.
Just like the bottle, we can all learn something,
that life brings circumstances that can make
us feel things we cannot compromise in.
We are bottled up inside with lots of things, but
only to know that sometimes we are drowning.
If we learn to spill and glide like the bottle
that holds the special things then all will
become easier to deal with from within.
We hold a lot inside our hearts, we hold a lot
inside of our minds and sometimes we ignore
the fact that we are special, inside.
We are created with greatness, but sometimes it can be too
late only to find that we never get the chance to relate.
If we take time to figure out what is going on, on the
inside, then we will realise that it is ok to float sometimes
in life, just as the bottle that holds the special things.

Don't Live Your Life In A Frame

Don't live your life in a frame.
It is a box that keeps you contained.
Expand your mind, give yourself a break.
Take a chance and be brave.
It is not about the speed of your existence.
It is about the experiences life gives.
It is not about how many stairs you climb.
It is about the next stairs you choose to climb.
When you start taking those first step upward,
then you will realise that the frame is just a mirror of your limitations.
Explore your thoughts beyond imagination.
You never know where life will take you, slow and easy, just where you need to be.
You will see that the frame is just a barrier.
You will see your fears.
A disguise, a misguided thing that keeps you contained in a frame.

The Shadow

The shadow is real although it doesn't stay complete.
The shadow comes and the shadow goes.
It becomes a friend when it wants to.
I remember as a child my shadow likes to play.
It moves when I move and do what I do.
The shadow becomes a friend, even at midnight too.
I think of the days when I feel lonely and blue.
My shadow was there to get me through.
It remains with you, even if you don't want it to.
It takes much more than your eyes to
see the shadow for what it is.
It takes appreciation to realise that
the shadow is a part of you.
It takes curiosity to be intrigued by
what the shadow shows to you.
When you look in the mirror and find your
shadow staring at you, the reflection you see
is the shadow that wants you to believe that
anything is possible and you can achieve.
Be the shadow you want to be.
It doesn't care.
It just wants you to be happy and carefree.

If I Should Go Crazy

If I should go crazy.
I know why.
I would know because my heart does not lie.
I would know that I should have listened to my thoughts that protects me from all sorts.
When life gets rough like the ocean.
When the sound of the sea wave roars.
When the darkness sets in the sky.
I would know that it is time to prepare for nature's calling but as it stands, I can compare my feelings to that scene because, with emotions overload, I do wonder if others think I feel.
I do wonder if others think I feel.
If I should wonder why I allowed myself to absorb nonsense in my life, I would know that it affect my spirit. I think of too much with so much rift, I spit out less of my 'goodness,' that I possess.

So, excuse me for wanting to rest my head from taking on the drama that the world spew on my conscience to make me think I am relating to normal when all I see is ignorance with no control, and a chaotic mess susceptible to profound arrogance and complete madness.

Excuse me for wanting my personal space, to breathe, to listen, to feel and to be in total silence to reside in my own space. I can hug my existence then.
At least I can feel what I am meant to feel and learn from my mistakes that suddenly becomes clear to me when I reflect. In that way I know I can avoid routine check-ups that take place in my head and affected my heart.

Excuse me for feeling like I want to escape to a world that lives within me and vanish from a world that will not give me the freedom, I so desire. I guess it can be a bubble, but deep down in my soul, I would know that reality can be a struggle, triggering my subconscious that defaulted my existence with illusions and consuming my mind with delusions, false hope and promises that do not relate to the realisation of what is real.

Excuse me for wanting to be free from the shackles that have gripped my mind, but in reality, that is what freedom means to me.

My Gut Never Lies To Me

My gut never lies to me.
Hot or cold, it rumbles and folds.
It curls with the intensity of my wellbeing.

I cannot decide if I am enough or should I let go of the feelings that
are gripping and teasing my subconscious?
>What do I do?
>What will I do?
>What shouldn't I do and what do I want to do?
>What can I do?

Emotions running wild, overload with doubts while feelings
evaporate and dissolve like ice while I accumulate all means to
function, confused and degenerating all my internal substance
and then eventually finding the energy to generate my source to
survive. Unsure, lack certainty but yet I am certainly attuned and
intact because my gut is questioning all that when I relate to all
these negatives holding me back.

The clenching feeling in my chest tells me, "You need to sort this
before you become a mess."
My heart says, "Yes if it feels right then that is the motion you
should address."
While my mind is telling me something else, my gut would be
saying,
"I digress as I am here to lead and to shield you from sadness!"

Follow me and listen when I speak to you as you will not be wrong
when I am in control of your intentions.
Take heed when you feel me as I am here to guide your feelings.
Don't be scared, that is why I am here to make you aware that I
care.

I Strum My Guitar Strings

When I strum the guitar.
Just a little string that says, ting!! Gives me chills.
When you know music, you will know what I mean.
You will be ready to sing when the strumming begins.
As I listen to the tune of the instrument, it becomes alive.
It makes you feel good, it makes you want to sing!
It refreshes your spirit and your mind is ready to take
control of the music when you start to sing from within.
Escape to a new dimension, new heights, elevation.
You forget your pain and you no longer want to sleep.
I seek solitude, healing with my thumbs
as I strum my guitar comfortably.
Lost in the moment, with the motion of stimulation.
My song has gripped me tremendously.
Where I feel no more pain, happiness
brings new meaning to me.
The sound of the music encourages me
to seek reflection and to be real.
I find comfort in singing melodiously,
with my soul at peace, I give in.
The story of my life I write and sing.
I give my time to creative thrills.
This is where my music sings as I strum my guitar strings.

An Open Heart

An open heart will allow you to feel things differently,
and just like the mind, it will see things too.
Abundance will flow through you if you allow your heart to do what it wants to.
It gives you opportunities to know others that are just
like you and who wants to keep life simple too.
It realises your dreams in different ways and open doors to you, but
only when one lets go of all animosity that one holds inside, not only for
themselves but for others too, which can sometimes be a hard thing to do.

Anger makes you weak, it doesn't make you stronger and can make you have
to work harder. It is not a good tool to use and it can turn you into a bad fool.
I tried it once, I tried it twice, even thrice, but it affected my life.
It did not work. I learnt that my heart needs to be opened for me
to see experiences with positivity and that an unforgiving heart
can make us escalate the things we do not need in our space.

Life doesn't have to be dormant and it doesn't have to be sad.
Even when you put a smile on your heavy heart, it changes the
way you think in that moment and happiness can be grand.
You can choose to give yourself a chance and heal at that
time while you ask for help from the Great Devine.

Love is all we need. We cannot live without it although we still breathe. If
your heart cannot live the life it sees then your body will be decease.
Give it a chance, it wants to beat its rhythm and do what it is meant to do but if
we fill our hearts with filth and junk then the chances are we will be that too.
The heart is an open gate to bring good things in. "So a man
thinketh so is he." So be careful of what you put in.

Vulnerability doesn't always have to be a bad thing. If
the heart is open it can show many things.
Truth comes to you when you listen to what your heart tells you and
acceptance will find you once you do. They say that "honesty is the
best policy," but if your heart is not honest, how can that be? If you
define what truth is; it is facts and events that happen for real.
So being true to self is the start of what is meant to be and an open heart
will help to get you started loving you the way you are supposed to.

Lonely People

*Many people in this world are suffering in silence
because their lonely tears never dry up.
There are many of us in this world that denies ourselves
peace of mind because our conscience never gives up.*

*There are a lot of lonely people in this world that feels like they
are not included in society because they may feel different about
their existence. They question themselves and they struggle
to fit in because they are trying to satisfy the masses.
Some people seek acceptance but get confused and fight
within themselves because they just cannot find it.
Some go to their beds at nights with tears in their eyes and with
the feeling of sadness; they wake up depressed because they
feel that no one cares and the world is against them.
There are those with high expectations but drenched their
pillows with teardrops all because they think that they
are a failure and their hard effort is not enough.*

*There are some people with big aspirations but give up hope
because of life setbacks and unexpected challenges.
Others go through emotional and mental turmoil because they have a
secret that they are ashamed to tell; while there are some with a serious
illness that they hide away from their family and best friends.*

*Many people cry tears even when they smile; you will never know
what is going on inside them because they are afraid to be open and
fear that they will be judged because of their previous choices.
Some may hold their tears in but with massive overload can
become a terrible manifestation, and the ones that seem ok choose
to blame them because they think they are so perfect.*

*Certain people want a start in life but don't know where to begin but
you will find a few people that are willing to share and help those
because they have felt the same thing. They will see that; because
they have walked a similar path in their lives but they are the few
because some people forgot that they can go down that road too.*

*It is never easy to tell a lonely person how to deal with their deflated
feelings, but if we as a people can reach out to others in a positive way,
then some lonely people could find it in themselves to be brave.
If we as a people that are in a better place in our lives can make
another lonely person feel appreciated then a little acknowledgement
can go a long way and help some lonely people who think that*

they don't matter and feel like others are just thoughtless.

Show Gratitude

Show gratitude.
It is not so hard.
With love in our hearts, with kindness, we part.
The things we do, we will always embark
on a life that karma can relate.
Life is not so hard when we appreciate the little things
that give us hope and put a simile on our face.
Be thankful for the hardest road, it is not the journey we
have to take but it is the lessons we need to appreciate.
Give yourself time to listen to your heart, and
think through your path before you start.

I Will Go Where The Wind Blows

I will go where the wind blows.
Where the wind blows with the rush.
The rush that greets the gush of rain.
The rain that pours while my skirt sways while the wind pulls me away.

Feeling the cold and icy mist on my skin.
The drops of crystals melt, and as I touch my head I feel raindrops there as
well while the wind pulls me in.

I will continue on my path.
The road seems long as the wind ruffles me on my way.
I know the choice is down to me so I am determined to continue along
through the day. I will let go instead, and let the wind lead me as I learn to
manoeuvre my way.

Now, I am flexible with my steps and I allow the wind to blow while I
gripped my toes in my shoes and stand steady while I rock to and fro. I can
sincerely say, I am learning to grow.

Staying grounded and firmly strong while I trodded on my path, I
imagined a life like the wind, with ups and downs and rocky steps, I see
the positive in my stride. There are times when I had to stop on my way
while the wind pushed and pulled me in various directions. My balance
is untamed but I found ways to keep grounded while the wind ruffles and
blow leaves in my face.

It was never easy to stand firm on my feet but I learnt to balance myself
anyway and trusted the wind to let me in. With that in thought, I have
taken from this journey a lesson learnt; the wind can come with a storm,
it can come with rain and sunshine too, so whatever life circumstances
may be thrown at us there will always be a way to deal with life's obstacles
once we choose.

Changing perceptions and looking at perspectives, I can finally say that
I have learnt something today while venturing out on a cold and rainy,
windy day.

My Pillow

While the pillow becomes a friend.
The dreams I share; my pillow cannot comprehend as I succumb to admit the life I lead is mine.
I give hope to much-needed thrills when all my dreams my pillow sees.
Sleepless nights and lonely days, my pillow caress my head and showed me care; giving me comfort as it may with assurance, I keep my love forever and always.

I take deep breaths and wrestle well with thoughts unseen but no events unfolding.
Despite my pillow setting me free, with questions in mind; I wondered when all my dreams will ever be. "Is it just a spell or is it just me!"My pillow dried my tears tirelessly and allow me to see myself in ways I wouldn't have imagined. My intention heals and the good it sees keeps me from drowning in the deep.

My pillow; my best friend listens and feel the pain my heart rebel but in time I see that making judgments does not help. I learn to see that it is not a purpose to be hard on myself.
With defiance, my pillow talk gave me that reflection, the comfort I gain from beyond and within. I know that life is a journey that I have trodden and a story I will tell.

Where life abounds, it prepares me not for the unseen but takes me through the motions as I seek the answers I cannot give. With my mind at ease and my strength resolved, my fears are gone with the clarity I surpass the challenges in my head. My courage has grown, I can see the light. I feel the doubts fading in the dark. So here I am radiant and strong. Thanks to my pillow that keeps me moving along.

The Trees

I like to hug the trees.
There is a connection we do not see.
It is not just about the green leaves in between.
They groom their branches in the seasons and shapeshift when there is a
reason. Autumn and winter; their colours are changed to bronze or gold,
and they shed their skin as they get old. Summer and spring, they are bold
with a makeover they grow, and become new and ready to be vibrant again
as they get rid of the old.

I like to hug the trees when they are old as I see their wisdom and much
more.
Their firm chunks have managed to see all that has been battered and thorn
when a storm sets in with the wind and the snow. You can tell that they have
endured many broken limbs, they get tattered and worn.

I like to hug the trees because they get ignored. I find peace when I do
as they also have a soul. They cannot speak to me but I can still hear,
sometimes they groan and you don't know. They remind me of old souls with
many years of life experience to show.

They can tell a good story just like the old folks and opened your mind to
ancient times. Their olden days are still reflected when you observe their
roots, you can see how they are affected by the good old days in their time.
Standing tall and firm as they do, with their pride intact you can see their
strength protruded to the skies as they elevated far and high.

I like to hug the trees, they are solid and strong. They may do things you
might not understand. They spread their branches in different directions
and give comfort to those who like to sit on their roots and appreciate their
existence. They know their purpose on the earth and where they grow they
cannot move. They must be humble to their soil as that is where they can get
their water to breathe and their food to feed, so they can have a life to live,
and the life they want to lead.

I cannot imagine my life as a tree, it wouldn't make sense to me, to be stuck
in one place all along and has to stretch to reach my destiny. I respect the
fact that trees are here to love me back. They provide a lot. As I see the need
for fresh air, I know the trees love me dear, and I love them back because
they care.

Why Cry

Why cry?
When life is so precious and you are breathing in it.
Why cry?
When all the wonders of this world are loving you, caressing and reaching out to you.
Why cry?
When the skies are blue and the stars, the moon, and the sunshine down on you.
Why cry?
When the features of this beautiful land are looking at you.
Why cry?
When the lush green bushes spread their buds in the wild forest and the freshwater flows from the Springs.
Why cry?
When the trees wave their branches and smile back at you.
Why cry?
When love is so abundantly waiting for you.
Why cry?
When you are also a part of this existence where life embraces you.
Why cry?
When all you need to do is, say thank you.
Why cry?
When all you need to say is, I love you.

The Writing On The Wall

The writing on the wall,
like graffiti, it will always tell a
story and it will not fall.
You can let your imagination go wild!
It doesn't have to be perfect.
As long as there is a meaning and you can reflect.
With not much to say, you can write it in any way.
An expression is like a story.
You can choose to tell it silently.
Even if you choose to write it on the wall.

The Rippled Water Flows

The rippled water flows and with the wind, it blows.
The fishes are swimming fervently in the pond they honed while they
are enjoying their home as the fresh spring waters flow home.

I take time to smell the roses while the day brightly glows, and as I
listen to the hummingbirds' chirps, they sing sweet music to my soul.
Here go the daffodils! spreading their leaves while drinking dews in the cold.
The lilies also are white and tall with their fresh vines protruding from
their moist soil, and I can see that they are enjoying their growth.
What a beauty they transcend as transitioning is at their core.

As I sit and wait on the wooden bench, I watch the hills embrace me a whole.
The heightened peak stares down at me and I see
destiny reaching its hands out to hold.
The sunny mountain seems hard to reach but in mind, it feels like an epitome
of life itself as to climb seem hard to do but I still feel I can make it if I try.
Although hardship comes to mind I tell myself it is not
true, telling myself I can't, would be a lie.

As I question my thoughts and contemplated my choices,
I rested while I think of where to go on my depart.
As there is not much more here to see, I trodded along
happily while peaceful thoughts approached me.
I enjoyed the moments of the morning thrill while I walked along the
pathway. I reflected on many things I see as I observe and take deep breaths
in; while I resonate within, I feel warm sunlight penetrating my skin.

The trees seem to be also saying things as they silently cave in, with their
sprighted buds and their garnished leaves it is obvious they are replenishing.
I feel like I am in heaven, I feel like I want to sleep as they
appear to be hugging me deeply underneath. Their roots are
strong and sturdy and I hug them like I am their baby.
With their tranquil energy flowing around, I feel protected and I feel free.
I hear whispers from way up high where I cannot see.

I can feel the love and it is not hard to see that
nature's wonders are appreciated by me.